S0-BAV-771

THAT'S LIFE, SNOOPY

by CHARLES M. SCHULZ

Selected cartoons from
Thompson Is In Trouble, Charlie Brown, Vol. 2

FAWCETT CREST • NEW YORK

THAT'S LIFE, SNOOPY

This book prepared especially for Fawcett Crest Books, a unit of CBS Publications, the Consumer Publishing Division of CBS Inc., comprises the second half of THOMPSON IS IN TROUBLE, CHARLIE BROWN, and is reprinted by arrangement with Holt, Rinehart and Winston, Inc.

ISBN: 0-449-23876-8

Printed in the United States of America

14   13   12

THAT'S LIFE, SNOOPY

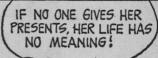

IF A BOY NEVER SENDS A GIRL FLOWERS, HE ROBS HIMSELF OF ONE OF THE GREAT JOYS OF LIFE...

THIEF! ROBBER!!

To Whom It May Concern;

Dear Whom,

THIS IS KIND OF INTERESTING... WOODSTOCK SAYS HE SORT OF FIGURED IT WAS A SCARECROW..

HE SAYS THAT HE KNEW ALL ALONG IT WASN'T A REAL HUMAN BEING BECAUSE MOST HUMAN BEINGS ARE NOT THAT FOND OF STANDING FOR SUCH A LENGTH OF TIME IN THE HOT SUN...

HE SAYS THE FACT THAT THE CLOTHES ARE OUT OF STYLE ALSO MADE HIM A LITTLE SUSPICIOUS..

BLEAH!

WOODSTOCK WOULD HAVE MADE A GOOD CROW!

ALL RIGHT, TEAM, LET'S PAY ATTENTION

WE'RE HERE TODAY TO TRY TO EVALUATE OUR PERFORMANCES ON THE FIELD...EACH OF US CAN STAND A LITTLE IMPROVEMENT...

EACH OF US CAN LEARN SOMETHING IF WE'RE WILLING TO ACCEPT CRITICISM...

YOUR NOSE IS TOO BIG!

Science Report;
"Forest Strangers"

Our wild life and our trees are protected by brave and dedicated men.

These men live by themselves in towers and are called Forest Strangers.

I WONDER IF I SHOULD INCLUDE AN EXPLANATION OF HOW THEY GOT THAT NAME..

PROBABLY NOT

HERE'S ONE FROM IOWA...AND HERE'S ONE FROM PENNSYLVANIA..

Advice For Dog Owners

type
type
type

"DEAR SIR, I HAVE A DOG WHO CONTINUALLY SCRATCHES HIS EARS...WHAT SHOULD I DO? SIGNED, 'WONDERING'"

Dear Wondering, What I'm wondering is how you can be so dumb! Take your dog to the vet right away, stupid.

type
type
type
type

"DEAR SIR, WE HAVE THREE PUPPIES WHO HAVE ENLARGED JOINTS AND ARE LAME... WHAT DO YOU THINK CAUSED THIS, AND WHAT SHOULD WE DO? SIGNED, 'DOG OWNER'"

Dear Dog Owner, Why don't you take up rock collecting? You're too stupid to be a dog owner. In the meantime, call your vet immediately.

type
type
type
type

"DEAR SIR, MY DOG HAS BEEN COUGHING LATELY... WHAT SHOULD I DO? SIGNED, 'CONFUSED'"

Dear Confused, You're not confused, you're just not very smart. Now, you get that dog to the vet right away before I come over and punch you in the nose!

type
type
type

I WRITE A VERY FIRM COLUMN!

WHAT A GREAT TITLE!

Toodle-oo, Caribou!
A Tale of the
Frozen North

One morning, Joe Eskimo went out to his barn to milk his polar cow. As he walked through the barn, tiny polar mice scampered across the frozen floor.

HMM..

type
type
type
type

Toodle-oo, Caribou!
A Tale of the
Frozen North

The stall was empty!
"Someone has stolen my
polar cow!" shouted Joe Eskimo.

"This is the work
of Joe Jacket,
who hates me!"

MAY I SEE HOW YOUR NEW NOVEL IS COMING ALONG?

BE MY GUEST..

"JOE ESKIMO AND JOE JACKET WERE RIVALS FOR THE HEART OF SALLY SNOW WHO LIVED SOUTH OF THE ICEBERG ...JOE ESKIMO THOUGHT BACK TO THE NIGHT HE FIRST SHOOK HER HAND"

"'I THINK YOU ARE VERY NICE,' HE HAD TOLD HER, AND THEY SHOOK HANDS."

THEY SHOOK HANDS?

I THINK YOUR LOVE SCENE NEEDS A LITTLE SOMETHING..

I ALWAYS GET SO EMBARRASSED..

ISN'T HE GOING TO SAY GOODBY?

WHEN YOU LEAVE ON AN ASSIGNMENT FOR THE HEAD BEAGLE, YOU DON'T HAVE TIME TO SAY GOODBY!

RIGHT!

"THOMPSON IS IN TROUBLE!" THAT MEANS I'VE GOT TO GET TO HIM BEFORE "THEY" DO...

THIS REMINDS ME OF THE "MOROCCAN AFFAIR"..THAT WAS A NASTY PIECE OF BUSINESS...

THAT STUPID THOMPSON...HE NEVER WANTED TO TAKE ANY ADVICE..NOW, MAYBE IT'S TOO LATE..

UH...IT'S LIKE THIS, SWEETIE...

I'M KIND OF LOOKING FOR A CHARACTER NAMED THOMPSON, SEE, AND I SORTA NEED YOUR HELP

HE'S ABOUT FOURTEEN INCHES... CARRIES A GOOD STRAIGHT LINE, HARKS TO THE TRACK, HAS A QUICK CLAIMING MOUTH RIGHT IN THE GROUND AND HAS A GOOD PEDIGREE

SHE KNOWS HIM!!

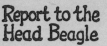
Report to the
Head Beagle

Subject: Our Beagle in
the field, Thompson.

Subject attempted to
subdue ten thousand
rabbits by himself. End
came quickly.

Rabbit-tat-tat, and
it was all over!

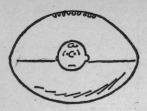

THERE'S THIS GIRL, SEE, AND SHE'S ALWAYS TRYING TO GET ME TO KICK THIS FOOTBALL, BUT SHE ALSO ALWAYS PULLS IT AWAY AND I LAND ON MY BACK AND KILL MYSELF...

SHE SOUNDS LIKE AN INTERESTING GIRL...SORT OF A FUN TYPE...

I GET THE IMPRESSION THAT YOU HAVE A REAL NEED TO KICK THIS FOOTBALL...I THINK YOU SHOULD TRY IT!

I THINK YOU SHOULD TRY IT BECAUSE IN MEDICAL TERMS, YOU HAVE WHAT WE CALL THE "NEED TO NEED TO TRY IT"

I'M GLAD I TALKED WITH MY PSYCHIATRIST BECAUSE THIS YEAR I'M GONNA KICK THAT BALL CLEAR TO THE MOON!

AUGH!

UNFORTUNATELY, CHARLIE BROWN, YOUR AVERAGE PSYCHIATRIST KNOWS VERY LITTLE ABOUT KICKING FOOTBALLS

HMM..

IT SAYS HERE THAT THE HUMMINGBIRD IS THE ONLY WINGED CREATURE THAT CAN FLAP HIS WINGS FAST ENOUGH TO BE ABLE TO HOVER MOTIONLESS IN THE AIR...

YES, MA'AM, WE'D LIKE TO SEE THE PRINCIPAL IF HE'S NOT TOO BUSY...

WELL, IT'S KIND OF A PERSONAL MATTER... YES, MA'AM... WE'RE STUDENTS HERE..

WHAT DID YOU THINK WE WERE, ENCYCLOPEDIA SALESMEN?

WHATEVER HAPPENED TO GOOD OLD-FASHIONED TACT?!

PRINCIPAL'S OFFICE

HOW CAN I WRITE MY ENGLISH THEME ON MISS SWEETSTORY'S NEW BOOK IF IT'S BEEN BANNED FROM OUR LIBRARY?

MAYBE YOU'LL HAVE TO WRITE ABOUT SOMETHING ELSE...

HOW ABOUT GRAPES?

I COULD WRITE ABOUT HOW EXCITING IT IS WHEN THE GRAPE BOATS COME SAILING INTO THE ARBOR...

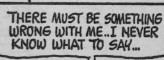

THERE MUST BE SOMETHING WRONG WITH ME..I NEVER KNOW WHAT TO SAY...

SCHOOL CROSSING

I'M MAD, CHARLIE BROWN!

THEY'VE BANNED HELEN SWEETSTORY'S BOOK FROM OUR SCHOOL LIBRARY, AND I CAN'T FIND OUT WHY!!

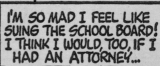

I'M SO MAD I FEEL LIKE SUING THE SCHOOL BOARD! I THINK I WOULD, TOO, IF I HAD AN ATTORNEY...

BEFORE I TAKE ANY CASE, I HAVE TO KNOW WHERE TO SEND THE BILL!

Dear Miss Sweetstory,
I suppose you have
heard about the banning
of your book from our library.

Well, I just wanted
you to know that I am
fighting for you. I
have even hired an attorney.

"THE SUPPRESSING OF EVIDENCE
OUGHT ALWAYS TO BE TAKEN FOR
THE STRONGEST EVIDENCE!"

Such as he is.

OKAY, ATTORNEY, LET'S MAKE A FEW PHONE CALLS, AND SEE WHAT WE CAN FIND OUT..

"WE KNOW THAT THE LAW IS GOOD IF A MAN USE IT LAWFULLY"

HELLO, SCHOOL BOARD?

I WONDER IF JOHN DOE OR RICHARD ROE WILL BE IN COURT... I HATE CASES THAT DON'T HAVE JOHN DOE OR RICHARD ROE..

YES, I'D LIKE TO SPEAK TO THE HEAD OF THE SCHOOL BOARD, PLEASE..

"THE CLIENT CARES LITTLE FOR A 'BEAUTIFUL' CASE"

SCHULZ

YOU WANT ME TO TALK TO MY OWN DOCTOR ABOUT MISS SWEETSTORY'S BOOK?

WHY NOT? HE'S ON THE SCHOOL BOARD, ISN'T HE? HE WAS THE ONE WHO BANNED HER BOOK!

DO PEOPLE REALLY TALK TO DOCTORS?

OF COURSE, CHARLIE BROWN.. EVERY DAY...

DO THE DOCTORS LISTEN?

OKAY, I HOPE YOU'RE SATISFIED... I TALKED WITH MY PEDIATRICIAN..

ACTUALLY, HE'S A VERY SENSITIVE PERSON...EVEN THOUGH HE FAINTS A LOT.... HE ADMITTED THAT HE'S NEVER REALLY READ MISS SWEETSTORY'S BOOK...

HE SAID HE ONLY READS MEDICAL JOURNALS...

ALTHOUGH SOMETIMES THE PICTURES UPSET HIM

DO YOU FEEL THAT THIS HAS BEEN ONE OF THOSE BRIGHT MOMENTS, CHUCK. DO YOU FEEL THAT THIS HOUR WE HAVE HAD TOGETHER HAS BEEN LIKE A DIAMOND SET IN A BRACELET?

DO YOU FEEL THAT WAY, CHUCK? IF YOU DO, YOU SHOULD TELL ME..

WHY, YES...I THINK YOU'RE RIGHT.. LIFE IS VERY MUCH LIKE A COLLAR..

NOT A COLLAR, CHUCK.. A BRACELET!!!

SPEAKING OF COLLARS, SWEETIE.. I'M AN EXPERT!

I REMEMBER ONCE BACK ABOUT FIVE YEARS AGO... I SAID THE RIGHT THING..

IS THERE A LOT OF SWEARING IN THIS MOVIE?

I DON'T WANT TO SEE IT IF THERE'S A LOT OF SWEARING.. I'M NOT IN THE ARMY, YOU KNOW!

I LIKE TO THINK OF MYSELF AS A LADY, AND I REFUSE TO GO TO A MOVIE THAT HAS A LOT OF SWEARING...

WHY DO YOU TAKE ME TO MOVIES THAT HAVE A LOT OF SWEARING?

I'M NOT TAKING YOU TO THE MOVIES

THERE ARE A LOT OF THINGS IN THIS WORLD THAT WOODSTOCK HAS NEVER SEEN...ONE OF THEM IS A SALT LICK!

Reason for writing Book _I wrote from a sense of need. I needed something to do. You can't just sleep all day long._

I was one of eight Beagles. We had a happy life. Lots to eat and a good cage, although looking out at the world through chicken wire can get to you after awhile.

Married _Almost once, but that's a long story._

Schools and Colleges attended _Obedience school dropout._

Suggestions for Promotion _If you don't promote my book, I'll get another publisher so fast it will make your head spin._

I LIKE FILLING OUT QUESTIONNAIRES!

"SOME MIGRATING BIRDS ARE GUIDED BY A SINGLE STAR"

"OTHERS ARE GUIDED IN THEIR TRAVELS BY LINES OF MAGNETIC FORCE"

STILL OTHERS TALK A STUPID FRIEND INTO GOING ALONG, AND SHOWING THEM THE WAY!

DO I KNOW WHAT YOU WOULD DO IF YOU HAD FORTY DOLLARS? NO, WHAT WOULD YOU DO IF YOU HAD FORTY DOLLARS?

BUY A FORTY-DOLLAR CANDY BAR!

HEE HEE HEE HEE HEE

I HATE JOKES LIKE THAT... I THINK THIS MIGRATING IS WARPING WOODSTOCK'S BRAIN!

IT'S GONE!! THE DAISY HILL PUPPY FARM IS GONE!

THEY'VE BUILT A SIX-STORY PARKING GARAGE! AAUGH! I CAN'T STAND IT!!

YOU STUPID PEOPLE!!

YOU'RE PARKING ON MY MEMORIES!!!

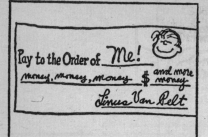

WOODSTOCK FEELS THAT EATING BREAD CRUMBS IS KIND OF DEGRADING...

WOODSTOCK THINKS THAT IF YOU SIT IN A MAILBOX LONG ENOUGH, YOU'LL GET A CHRISTMAS CARD..HE'S SO NAIVE...HE JUST..

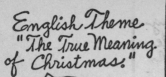

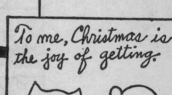

➡

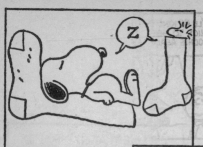

IF SHE COMES WITHIN A THOUSAND MILES OF ME, I'LL SCREAM!

IT'LL BE KIND OF NICE TO SEE POOCHIE AGAIN

SEEING POOCHIE AGAIN WOULD BE LIKE GETTING THE MUMPS TWICE!

YOU'VE NEVER FORGIVEN HER HAVE YOU?

YOU DON'T FORGIVE SOMEONE WHO DOES TO YOU WHAT SHE DID TO ME!

ANYWAY, HERE'S THE CARD..

I'LL BET SHE DOESN'T EVEN REMEMBER WHAT HAPPENED..

THAT WOULD BE JUST LIKE HER NOT TO REMEMBER...SHE'LL COME TO SEE ME, TOO... I KNOW SHE WILL..

JUST WHAT I DIDN'T NEED...A POOCHIE CHRISTMAS!

POOCHIE'S HERE! SHE WANTS TO SEE YOU

I DON'T WANT TO SEE HER...NOT AFTER WHAT SHE DID TO ME..

THAT WAS A LONG TIME AGO..

I DON'T CARE... WE BEAGLES HAVE MEMORIES LIKE BEAGLES!

" THERE I WAS, AN INNOCENT LITTLE PUPPY, BOUNCING AROUND THE YARD ONE DAY...EAGER TO PLEASE...WILLING TO DO ANYTHING FOR A LITTLE AFFECTION ... "

➤

"THEN THIS LITTLE GIRL COMES ALONG...'POOCHIE' WAS HER NAME..SHE HAD A STICK IN HER HAND"

"'HI, CUTE PUPPY!' SHE SAYS. 'DO YOU WANT TO CHASE THE STICK?'"

"SO SHE THROWS THE STICK, AND I, LIKE A FOOL, GO RUNNING AFTER IT..."

"...FALLING ALL OVER MYSELF, BUMPING MY NOSE AND GETTING A MOUTHFUL OF MUD..."

" I GO RUNNING BACK WITH THE STICK, BRIGHT AND EAGER.."

"..JUST IN TIME TO SEE HER WALKING AWAY WITH AN ENGLISH SHEEP DOG!"

I'M AMAZED THAT YOU REMEMBER ALL THAT

HOW COULD I FORGET?

I STILL HAVE THE STICK!

I JUST WANTED TO THANK YOU AGAIN FOR THE STRING OF PEARLS YOU GAVE ME FOR CHRISTMAS...

I DID NOT GIVE YOU A STRING OF PEARLS FOR CHRISTMAS..

I'LL SAY YOU DIDN'T!

QUESTION NUMBER ONE...

TRUE!

TRUE AGAIN! FALSE!

TRUE, BY GOLLY! AND FALSE AND TRUE AND TRUE!

FALSE AGAIN!! THERE'S NO DOUBT ABOUT IT!

➤

PEANUTS

YOU'RE A PAL, SNOOPY!
(selected cartoons from
You Need Help Charlie Brown, Vol. 2) 23775 $1.25

PLAY BALL, SNOOPY
(selected cartoons from
Win a Few, Lose a Few, Charlie Brown, Vol. 1) 23222 $1.50

YOU'VE GOT TO BE KIDDING, SNOOPY!
(selected cartoons from
Speak Softly and Carry a Beagle, Vol. 1) 23453 $1.25

HERE'S TO YOU, CHARLIE BROWN
(selected cartoons from
You Can't Win, Charlie Brown, Vol. 2) 23708 $1.25

GOOD GRIEF, CHARLIE BROWN!
(selected cartoons from
Good Grief, More Peanuts! Vol. 1) 23801 $1.50

Buy them at your local bookstore or use this handy coupon for ordering.

COLUMBIA BOOK SERVICE (a CBS Publications Co.)
32275 Mally Road, P.O. Box FB, Madison Heights, MI 48071

Please send me the books I have checked above. Orders for less than 5 books must include 75¢ for the first book and 25¢ for each additional book to cover postage and handling. Orders for 5 books or more postage is FREE. Send check or money order only.

Cost $_____ Name _____

Sales tax*_____ Address _____

Postage_____ City _____

Total $_____ State _____ Zip _____

* The government requires us to collect sales tax in all states except AK, DE, MT, NH and OR.